Awesome
Animal
Skills

Wolves and Other
Animals
That
Outrun Prey

Vic Kovacs

WINDMILL
BOOKS

New York

Published in 2016 by **Windmill Books**,
an Imprint of Rosen Publishing
29 East 21st Street, New York, NY 10010

Developed and produced for Rosen by BlueAppleWorks Inc.

Art Director: T.J. Choleva
Managing Editor for BlueAppleWorks: Melissa McClellan
Designer: Joshua Avramson
Photo Research: Jane Reid
Editor: Marcia Abramson

Photo Credits:
Cover left, p. 6 top left Cynthia Kidwell/Shutterstock; cover, p. 5 Bildagentur Zoonar GmbH/Shutterstock; back cover, p. 14-15 Petr Podrouzek/Shutterstock; title page weisen007/Thinkstock; TOC top David Dohnal/Shutterstock;TOC bottom Francois van Heerden/Shutterstock; p. 4 top left Maria Jeffs/Shutterstock; p. 4 top Zheltyshev/Shutterstock; p.4 left MartieGoddard/Thinkstock; p 4-5 Scott E Read/Shutterstock; p. 6 top Holly Kuchera/Shutterstock; p. 6 Jeannette Katzir Photog/Shutterstock; p. 7 marikond/Shutterstock; p. 8 top left Purestock/Thinkstock; p. 8 top Marcella Miriello/Shutterstock; p. 8 kochanowski/Shutterstock; p. 9outdoorsman/Shutterstock; p. 9 top ValerijaP/Thinkstock;p. 10 top left Fuse/Thinkstock; p. 10 top GryT/Shutterstock; p. 10 right Tom Tietz/Thinkstock; p. 10-11 Fuse/Shutterstock; P. 11 Lori Labrecque/Shutterstock; p. 12 top left Vladimir Kogan Michael/Shutterstock; p. 12 top David Dohnal/Shutterstock; p. 12 yykkaa/Shutterstock; p. 12-13 Vladimir Kogan Michael/Shutterstock; p. 13 Giedriius/Shutterstock; p. 14 top left TTstudio/Shutterstock; p. 14 top JCREATION/Shutterstock; p. 14 left Anatolich/Shutterstock; p. 15 right surawutob/Shutterstock; p. 16 top left Chris Hill/Shutterstock; p. 16 top mlorenz/Shutterstock; p. 16 left Ronnie Howard/Shutterstock;p. 16-17 Thomas Barrat/Shutterstock; p. 16 right DnDavis/Shutterstock;p. 17 Feng Yu/Shutterstock; p. 18 top left stockpix4u/Shutterstock; p. 18 top Kim Briers/Shutterstock; p. 18-19 AH Design Concepts/Thinkstock; p. 19 Beverly Speed/Shutterstock; p. 20 top left Nick Biemans/Shutterstock; p. 20 top Ewan Chesser/Shutterstock; p. 20Daleen Loest/Shutterstock; p. 21 top Ablestock.com/Thinkstock; p. 21 bottom Sean Nel/Shutterstock; p. 22 top left Brandon Alms/Shutterstock; p. 22 top Matee Nuserm/Shutterstock; p. 22-23 AzriSuratmin/Shutterstock; p. 23 Sebastian Janicki/Shutterstock; p. 24 top left Anusorn999/Dreamstime; p. 24 top, 24-25 Lai Wagtail/Shutterstock; p 24 right Sergiy Goruppa/Thinkstock; p. 25 bottom Siriporn Schwendener/Shutterstock; p. 25 Shih-Hao Liao/Thinkstock; p. 26 top left Yatra/Shutterstock; p. 26 top Nick Fox/Shutterstock; p. 26 costas anton dumitrescu/Shutterstock; p. 26 right Aberson/Dreamstime; p. 27 Jezbennett/Shutterstock;p. 28 top left Don Fink/Shutterstock; p. 28 top Gary Leive/Thinkstock; p. 28 middle Wizreist/Dreamstime; p. 28-29 Tilmann von Au/Thinkstock.

Cataloging-in-Publication-Data

Kovacs, Vic.
Wolves and other animals that outrun prey / by Vic Kovacs.
p. cm. — (Awesome animal skills)
Includes index.
ISBN 978-1-4777-5657-7 (pbk.)
ISBN 978-1-4777-5656-0 (6 pack)
ISBN 978-1-4777-5588-4 (library binding)
1. Wolves — Juvenile literature. 2. Animal behavior — Juvenile literature.
3. Predatory animals — Juvenile literature. I. Title.
QL737.C22 K68 2016
599.773—d23

Manufactured in the United States of America
CPSIA Compliance Information: Batch #WS15WM: For Further Information contact: Rosen Publishing, New York, New York at 1-800-237-9932

CONTENTS

OUTRUNNING THE PREY

Endurance hunting takes much energy on the hunter's part. At the end, the predator is left exhausted itself.

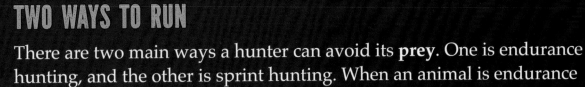

TWO WAYS TO RUN

There are two main ways a hunter can avoid its **prey**. One is endurance hunting, and the other is sprint hunting. When an animal is endurance hunting its prey, it doesn't actually need to be faster. It just needs to last longer. The prey is often much faster than the **predator**, but the predator is able to keep a steady pace over long distances. This causes the prey to become exhausted. The hunter is then able to strike and catch the tired prey.

Sprint hunting is more about pure speed. Animals are able to produce great bursts of speed, during which they can quickly overtake their prey and finish them, usually with one quick strike. Sprint hunters include most of the fastest animals in the world, such as cheetahs.

Cheetahs are sprint hunters. This also requires a lot of energy, but it takes much less time than endurance hunting.

5

MYSTICAL WOLVES

Wolves use barks, howls, growls, and whimpers to communicate. Howling, for example, means "we are here."

Wolves are canines, a family of animals that also includes coyotes and jackals. Another notable relative is the domestic dog. Wolves and humans have had a long and complicated relationship. They are an ancestor of the modern dog, so we wouldn't have man's best friend without them. However, with their predatory nature, wolves have often been thought of as nuisances. They have been known to hunt and kill livestock. They are also often thought of as man-eaters, though in reality they are rarely dangerous to humans. Because of their long association with people, they are important figures in many ancient folktales and legends.

FAMILY LIFE

The gray wolf was once found all over North America, Europe, Asia, and even Africa. In many places the populations were wiped out to make the areas safer for humans and livestock. Wolves are social animals, living in groups called packs. Each pack is made up of one alpha male and one alpha female, who are the leaders. They are also mates, often for life, and are usually the only pair in the pack that breed. The rest of the pack is generally made up of their children, who will leave the pack once they are old enough, or if they come into conflict with the alphas. New packs are formed when a mature male and female who have left their families meet and come together to find a new territory.

Wolves can vary greatly in color, even within the same litter. Light gray, brown, and whitish coats are the norm, but all black or pure white wolves are not uncommon.

LANKY AND STRONG

Wolves are pretty big animals. They are well built to be able to outrun their prey. Their bodies are sleek, and they are very long-legged compared to other canines. These **adaptations** help them travel quickly through areas with plentiful snow. Males grow between two to three feet (0.6 to 0.9 m) tall. Females are slightly smaller. Males generally weigh about 100 pounds (45 kg), with females weighing about 15 to 20 pounds (7 to 9 kg) less. Habitat also plays a factor. Wolves living farther north are usually larger than their southern relatives. Both have incredibly powerful jaws, with 42 teeth that are perfectly evolved for tearing and processing meat.

Wolf fur has adapted to cold climates. It keeps the wolf warmer than dog fur would and resists ice buildup.

HUNGRY LIKE A WOLF

Wolves are opportunistic **carnivores**, meaning they usually eat whatever meat is around and easiest to get. They will eat small rodents such as mice and rats, and larger animals such as beavers and raccoons. Their favorite prey, though, are large hoofed mammals such as moose, deer, and caribou. They are also known to occasionally eat nuts and berries, but they could not survive on a diet of these alone. Though they are famous for being skilled hunters, wolves are also **scavengers**, and will gladly eat animals that have already died from other causes, like old age.

Some wolves are able to eat as much as 20 pounds (9 kg) of meat in one meal.

9

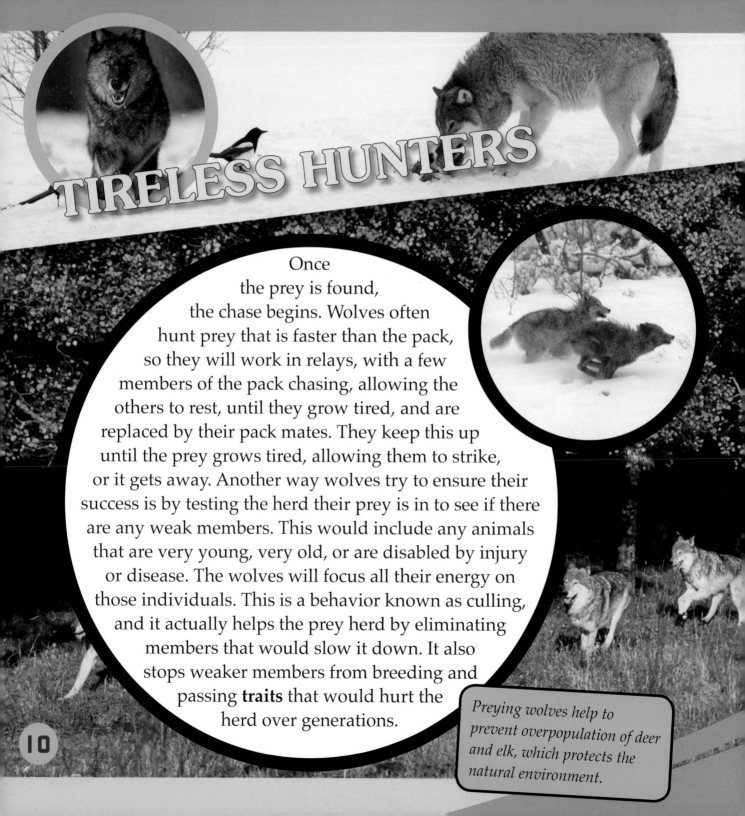

Once the prey is found, the chase begins. Wolves often hunt prey that is faster than the pack, so they will work in relays, with a few members of the pack chasing, allowing the others to rest, until they grow tired, and are replaced by their pack mates. They keep this up until the prey grows tired, allowing them to strike, or it gets away. Another way wolves try to ensure their success is by testing the herd their prey is in to see if there are any weak members. This would include any animals that are very young, very old, or are disabled by injury or disease. The wolves will focus all their energy on those individuals. This is a behavior known as culling, and it actually helps the prey herd by eliminating members that would slow it down. It also stops weaker members from breeding and passing **traits** that would hurt the herd over generations.

Preying wolves help to prevent overpopulation of deer and elk, which protects the natural environment.

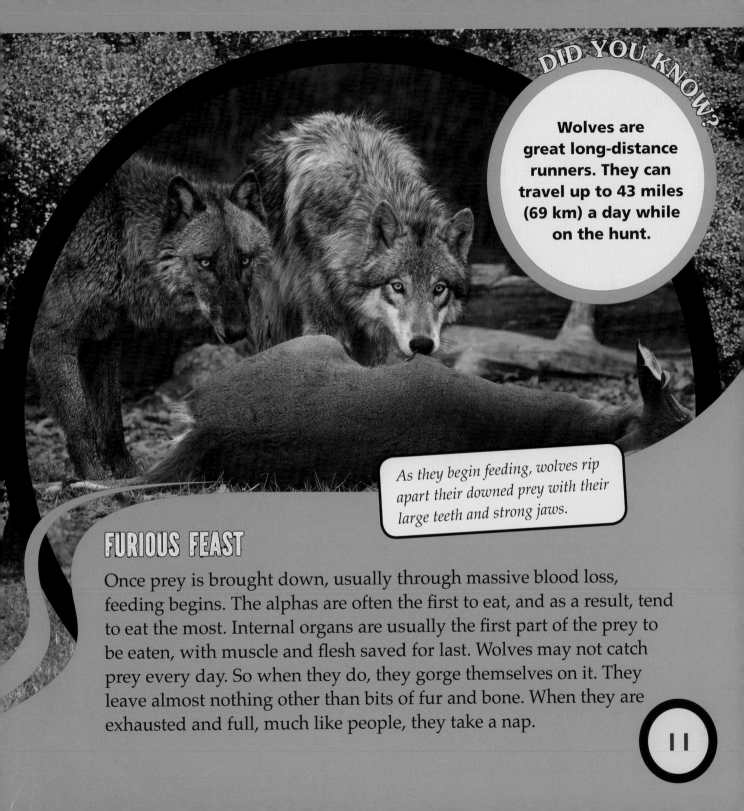

Wolves are great long-distance runners. They can travel up to 43 miles (69 km) a day while on the hunt.

As they begin feeding, wolves rip apart their downed prey with their large teeth and strong jaws.

FURIOUS FEAST

Once prey is brought down, usually through massive blood loss, feeding begins. The alphas are often the first to eat, and as a result, tend to eat the most. Internal organs are usually the first part of the prey to be eaten, with muscle and flesh saved for last. Wolves may not catch prey every day. So when they do, they gorge themselves on it. They leave almost nothing other than bits of fur and bone. When they are exhausted and full, much like people, they take a nap.

SOARING GOLDEN EAGLES

American golden eagles are found all over Canada, the western United States, and even as far south as central Mexico. They live in open spaces such as prairies and **tundra**, and they are often seen making their nests on rocky mountainsides. They are a deep brown in color, with their name coming from the golden feathers on the back of the neck. Golden eagles are one of the largest **raptors** in North America, with a wingspan that can reach seven feet (2.1 m). They usually live alone or with a mate, and have been known to mate for life.

Golden eagles are admired for their power. They are national symbols of several countries, including Mexico.

DEATH FROM ABOVE

Golden eagles are one of the fastest birds on earth. Once they spot prey from the sky, they are capable of diving at speeds of more than 150 miles per hour (241 km/h). Keeping a careful eye on their prey, which mostly consists of medium-sized mammals such as rabbits and prairie dogs, they can suddenly change course depending on which way the prey is trying to escape. They are also capable of striking other birds at such amazing speeds that they are actually knocked out of the sky.

Golden eagles prey mostly on small mammals, such as this red fox. Mammals make up more than 60 percent of their diet, perhaps because they cannot fly away!

With its powerful **talons** and beak, the golden eagle can hunt animals as big as caribou and sheep.

FAST-FLYING DRAGONFLIES

Dragonflies are brightly colored flying insects. They live near water all over the world, especially in tropical areas. Dragonflies have four wings and long, stick-like bodies. These wings are attached by separate muscles, unlike in most winged insects. These unique muscles give dragonflies unmatched wing control, giving them a range of abilities absent in most other flying insects. Their huge **compound eyes** allow them to see in almost every angle around them.

A dragonfly sees better than people do. Its compound eyes contain 30,000 light receptors and cover most of its head.

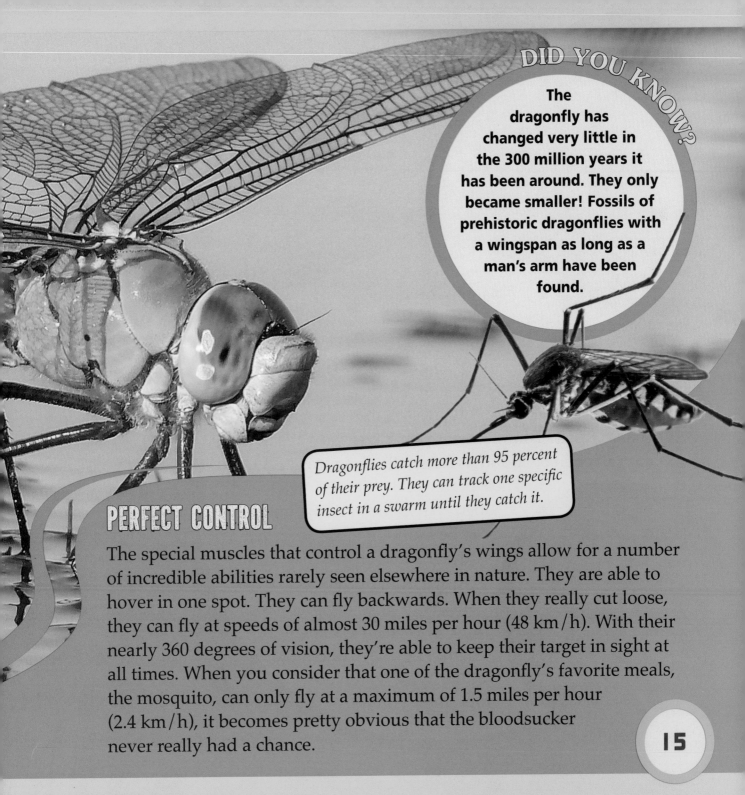

The dragonfly has changed very little in the 300 million years it has been around. They only became smaller! Fossils of prehistoric dragonflies with a wingspan as long as a man's arm have been found.

Dragonflies catch more than 95 percent of their prey. They can track one specific insect in a swarm until they catch it.

PERFECT CONTROL

The special muscles that control a dragonfly's wings allow for a number of incredible abilities rarely seen elsewhere in nature. They are able to hover in one spot. They can fly backwards. When they really cut loose, they can fly at speeds of almost 30 miles per hour (48 km/h). With their nearly 360 degrees of vision, they're able to keep their target in sight at all times. When you consider that one of the dragonfly's favorite meals, the mosquito, can only fly at a maximum of 1.5 miles per hour (2.4 km/h), it becomes pretty obvious that the bloodsucker never really had a chance.

15

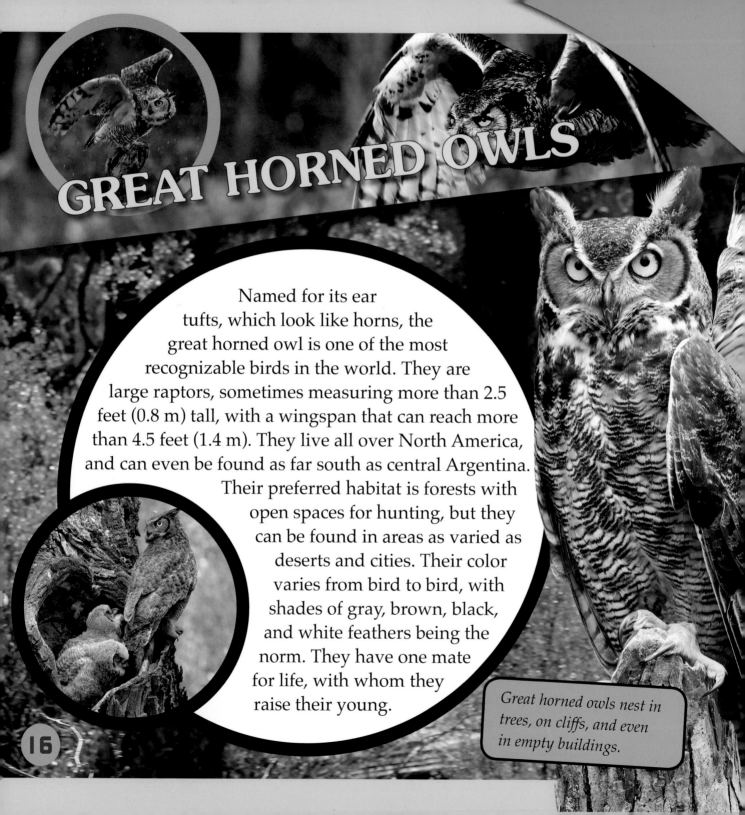

Named for its ear tufts, which look like horns, the great horned owl is one of the most recognizable birds in the world. They are large raptors, sometimes measuring more than 2.5 feet (0.8 m) tall, with a wingspan that can reach more than 4.5 feet (1.4 m). They live all over North America, and can even be found as far south as central Argentina. Their preferred habitat is forests with open spaces for hunting, but they can be found in areas as varied as deserts and cities. Their color varies from bird to bird, with shades of gray, brown, black, and white feathers being the norm. They have one mate for life, with whom they raise their young.

Great horned owls nest in trees, on cliffs, and even in empty buildings.

QUIET KILLERS

From small rodents to larger mammals such as skunks, and even other owls, the great horned owl is happy to eat whatever is available. Their favorite method of hunting is to sit on a high perch and wait for prey to pass by. They will also glide silently over open spaces, with wing feathers that are specially adapted to eliminate noise. Using their excellent night vision and incredible hearing, they can locate prey with ease. Once it is found, the owl will dive-bomb towards it, folding its wings into its body so it drops as quickly as possible to outfly the prey. When the owl is directly above its victim, it will strike with powerful talons that crush the life out of prey with almost thirty pounds (13.6 kg) of force.

Owls like to eat their prey whole, bones and all. If the prey is too big, they will tear it into smaller pieces.

BOLD PEACOCK MANTIS SHRIMP

The peacock mantis shrimp is one of the most unique and amazing animals on earth. They are eye-catching shades of green, red, orange, and blue, with spots on the arms and the shell around the head. They live in **burrows** they dig around coral reefs in the Indo-Pacific Ocean, which they protect fiercely. They typically measure from one to seven inches (2.5 to 18 cm). Their eyes are capable of seeing ten times as much color as a person. They actually see the most color of any animal in the world. They use this ability to avoid the fish that eat them and find the **crustaceans** and **mollusks** that make up their diet.

This spectacular shrimp gets its name from rainbow-colored peacock birds.

DID YOU KNOW?

Many aquariums won't keep peacock mantis shrimp because they are able to punch through the glass in their tanks.

POWER PUNCH

Unlike the other animals mentioned in this book, the peacock mantis shrimp doesn't outrun its prey with its whole body. It does it with just one limb. The peacock mantis shrimp is the proud owner of the fastest punch on earth. It is able to extend its blunt, club-like claws at a speed of more than 50 miles an hour (80.5 km/h). It is so powerful that it can easily smash the shell of a crab, breaking it into pieces. In fact, the mantis shrimp doesn't even need to hit its prey directly. This is because its punch is so fast and powerful that it creates an underwater shockwave with so much force that it is capable of killing. These amazing feats of strength and speed allow the peacock mantis shrimp to often go after prey much larger than itself, making it one of the most unusual and interesting hunters in the world.

DETERMINED AFRICAN WILD DOGS

Unlike other species of dogs, African wild dogs only have four toes instead of the normal five.

African wild dogs are also known as painted dogs because of their splotchy coats. These coats contain a number of different colors, with browns, reds, blacks, and whites being among the most common. They are about the size of a midsize domestic dog. They are very social animals, living in packs of between six and 20 animals. They are most common in southern Africa, although there are also populations in the southeast part of the continent. They generally prefer **savanna** and other open areas, which helps to make their hunts easier.

PACK PREDATORS

Like the wolf, African wild dogs often focus their hunt on prey that might be sick or otherwise disabled. The leader of the pack will focus all its attention on such an individual and the hunt starts. African wild dogs are among the fastest dogs. They can run as fast as 45 miles an hour (72 km/h). That still isn't fast enough to outrun much of their prey, so they instead rely on their incredible **stamina**, and cooperation within the pack. Most of the hunts last for about two miles, with the dogs slowly tiring out their prey over that distance. If the dog keeping pace with the prey itself becomes tired, it will fall back and another member of the pack will take its place. If the prey is too large to be brought down with a single attack, the dogs will nip at it repeatedly until it collapses from blood loss. One of the most efficient large carnivores, African wild dogs rarely allow prey to escape once the chase has begun.

Packs hunt antelopes and will also tackle much larger prey, such as zebras.

21

FAST-FLYING ROBBER FLIES

With more than 7,000 species, robber flies come in a wide variety of shapes and sizes. Their large compound eyes, placed on the sides of their heads, give them excellent eyesight. They have a small knife-like beak called a **proboscis** that functions as their mouth and their main weapon against prey. They are found all over the world, mostly in open areas with plentiful flowers, which attract some of their favorite prey species.

Robber flies wait to ambush prey, just as human robbers might. That is how they got their name.

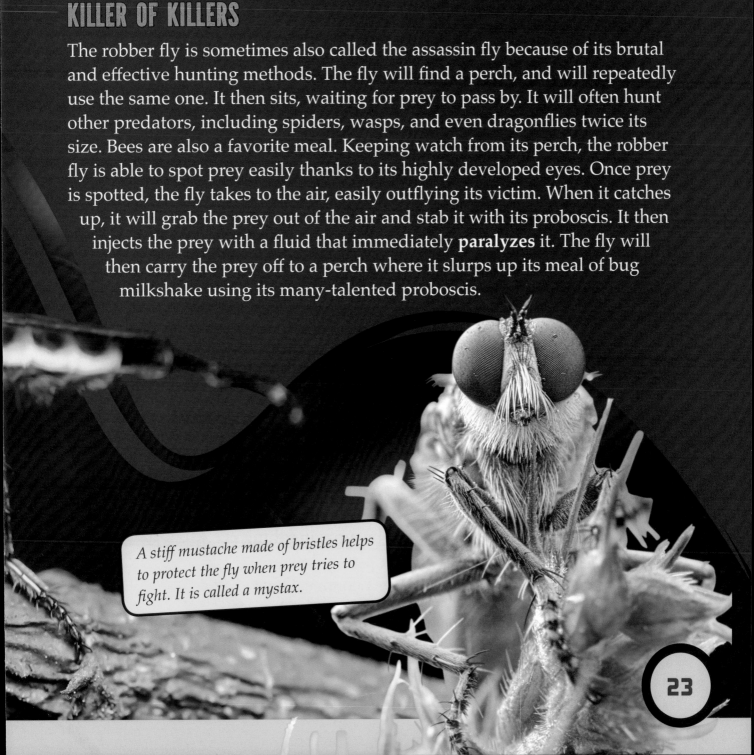

KILLER OF KILLERS

The robber fly is sometimes also called the assassin fly because of its brutal and effective hunting methods. The fly will find a perch, and will repeatedly use the same one. It then sits, waiting for prey to pass by. It will often hunt other predators, including spiders, wasps, and even dragonflies twice its size. Bees are also a favorite meal. Keeping watch from its perch, the robber fly is able to spot prey easily thanks to its highly developed eyes. Once prey is spotted, the fly takes to the air, easily outflying its victim. When it catches up, it will grab the prey out of the air and stab it with its proboscis. It then injects the prey with a fluid that immediately **paralyzes** it. The fly will then carry the prey off to a perch where it slurps up its meal of bug milkshake using its many-talented proboscis.

A stiff mustache made of bristles helps to protect the fly when prey tries to fight. It is called a mystax.

FAST-RUNNING TIGER BEETLES

Tiger beetles can run 120 times their body length in a single second. If a human being were to run 120 body lengths in a second, they would be running at a speed of around 480 miles an hour (773 km/h). This creates a unique problem for tiger beetles, because even though they have very strong eyes, they run so quickly they actually go blind. This is because they are running so fast their eyes can't take in images, and because the images they are getting are changing so quickly their brains can't process it. As a result, they have a unique hunting pattern of sprinting after prey, stopping to look around and get their bearings, and then sprinting towards the prey again. The amazing thing is that even with this starting and stopping they are so fast that most prey doesn't have a chance. Once the prey is caught, it is easily ripped apart by the tiger beetle's powerful jaws, called mandibles.

Unless they are being handled, tiger beetles don't bite humans. Their bites can sting!

Tiger beetles can live almost anywhere, from the tops of mountains to lakeshores to sand dunes.

With around 2,600 species, tiger beetles occur in dozens of different sizes and colors. Many species are bright and eye-catching, making them popular with bug collectors.

LAUGHING HYENAS

Hyena cubs live in underground dens with many tunnels. They hide in the tunnels if predators attack while their mothers are out hunting for food.

Hyenas resemble dogs, though they are actually more closely related to cats. There are three subspecies, the largest of which is the spotted hyena. They can measure almost five feet (1.5 m) long. Males are slightly smaller than females. They live in family-based groups called clans, which make their homes in dens. For live prey, they enjoy zebras, wildebeests, and antelopes. They live all over Africa in habitats that include savanna, grasslands, mountains, and wooded areas.

The hyena's "laugh" is actually a warning cry that can be heard from three miles (4.8 km) away.

Hyenas get as much as 75 percent of their food from hunting. They also raid places where people store food.

NOT STRICTLY SCAVENGERS

Typically thought of as scavengers, hyenas are also gifted hunters. They use many of the same techniques as their fellow African predator, the African wild dog. The clan often focuses on very young, very old, or unhealthy members of a herd. Separating one of these weakened members, the clan doggedly chases it over long distances, stealing a bite whenever they get close enough. Once the prey collapses, usually from a combination of shock and blood loss, the clan converges on it as one, with individuals often bickering over the available meat. After the bloody feast, not even bones are left.

SPEEDY ROADRUNNERS

Although it isn't as large or as colorful as its cartoon counterpart, the greater roadrunner is still a fascinating bird. Roadrunners live in deserts and open country in the American Southwest and as far south as central Mexico. They are mostly dark brown, with lines of lighter feathers, and a light underbelly. They measure up to two feet (0.6 m) from beak to tail, and usually don't weigh much more than a pound (0.45 kg). Roadrunners have unique x-shaped footprints, with two toes each in the front and the back, which make it almost impossible to tell which way it was headed. They get their names from often suddenly darting across roads, usually in the pursuit of prey.

When seeking a mate, male roadrunners will parade, bow, coo, and offer gifts such as food or twigs.

RUN, DON'T FLY

Roadrunners can fly, but they prefer to run, as they are much better at it. Far from a picky eater, the roadrunner is happy to eat whatever it can catch, and there isn't much it can't. Snakes, lizards, insects, small mammals, and even other birds all make up the roadrunner's diet. They are able to eat many poisonous species without a problem. Roadrunners often hunt by scaring prey out of hiding places by flashing their wings, making them appear large and frightening. If the roadrunner doesn't capture the prey right away, then the chase begins. Roadrunners can run at speeds of more than 15 miles an hour (24 km/h), keeping their bodies almost flat to the ground. Once they catch up to the prey, they snatch it with their beak. If small enough, it is swallowed in one gulp. If the meal is too large, the roadrunner will slam it onto a rock or the ground. This both finishes the prey off, and smashes it into a shape that is more easily swallowed by the roadrunner.

DID YOU KNOW?

Despite what you may have seen in cartoons, a roadrunner can't actually outrun a coyote. In fact, in real life, coyotes are about twice as fast as roadrunners.

GLOSSARY

ADAPTATIONS Changes that help an animal or plant adjust to its environment.

BURROW An underground hole, tunnel, or series of tunnels dug by an animal.

CARNIVORE A meat eater.

COMPOUND EYES A type of eye common in insects, made up of many repeating receptor units that allow them to see in wide angles.

CRUSTACEAN An animal with a body made up of sections covered by a hard shell, such as a lobster.

MOLLUSK An animal that has a soft body and usually lives in a shell, such as a clam.

PARALYZE To make immobile or unable to move.

PREDATOR Any animal that hunts and feeds on other animals.

PREY Any animal that is hunted and eaten by other animals.

PROBOSCIS A long, nose-like appendage used for feeding in many insects.

RAPTOR A meat-eating, predatory bird.

RECEPTOR A part of the body that senses light, sound, and other stimuli.

SAVANNA An area of grassland with few trees.

SCAVENGER An animal that will eat meat that it has found that has already been killed by something else.

STAMINA Staying power, endurance.

TALON A sharp, grasping claw, especially found on birds of prey such as owls or eagles.

TRAITS A quality or ability, often one that is passed from one generation to the next.

TUNDRA A type of habitat known for its cold temperatures and few trees.

FOR MORE INFORMATION

Further Reading

Brandenburg, Jim. *Face to Face with Wolves*.
Des Moines, IA: National Geographic Children's Books, 2010.

Read, Tracy. *Exploring the World Of Eagles*.
Buffalo, NY: Firefly Books, 2010.

Seidensticker, John. *Predators*.
New York, NY: Simon & Schuster Books for Young Readers, 2008.

Spelman, Lucy. *National Geographic Animal Encyclopedia*.
Des Moines, IA: National Geographic Children's Books, 2012.

WEBSITES

For web resources related to the subject of this book, go to:
www.windmillbooks.com/weblinks and select this book's title.

INDEX